# CHARLES MANSON

*A Life From Beginning to End*

Copyright © 2018 by Hourly History.

All rights reserved.

# Table of Contents

Introduction
Manson's Early Life
Becoming Charles Manson
Starting the Manson Family
Seeking Fame in Los Angeles
Spahn Ranch and Helter Skelter
The First Murder
10050 Cielo Drive
Rosemary and Leno LaBianca
Catching Charles Manson
Life and Death Behind Bars
Conclusion

# Introduction

In his early days as a cult leader, Charles Manson attracted young men and women to him with a message of peace and love. Sitting cross-legged on the grass, Manson played his guitar and sang songs about dropping acid and finding freedom—appealing ideas for a generation of young people who felt they had no place in straight society. All he wanted, Manson said, was to take care of the children the world had discarded.

The blossoming hippie counter-culture of the Haight-Ashbury district of San Francisco was fertile ground for Manson to collect followers. Thanks to Manson's unflinching confidence in his own rambling manifesto, he was able to prey on vulnerable young girls. Manson offered spiritual guidance and protection to the runaways in his care, and all he asked for in return was complete submission to his will.

Manson's so-called family believed every word he said and lived their lives in accordance with his whims. Yet the family's dream of freedom, love, and peace on earth lasted only as long as it took the drugs to wear off. Manson's guise as a spiritual leader, musician, and caretaker slipped away to reveal a madness that led to murder; in no time, the Manson Family dream transformed from an experiment in communal living and an attempt to live off the land to a nightmare of death and destruction.

Using a bizarre mixture of sources including advice from pimps he met in jail, Dale Carnegie's *How to Win*

*Friends and Influence People,* and pop music lyrics, Manson was able to convince his family to share his psychopathic thoughts and to eventually turn those thoughts into deeds. At his command, members of the Manson Family killed nine people. The motivation behind the murders was senseless, and the violence was extreme.

The Manson Family sustained Manson's ego and his delusions, but they did not create him. A neglected child, institutionalized by the prison system before he reached adulthood, Manson was a broken person who took advantage of a cultural movement to manipulate vulnerable and potentially mentally ill people to his own ends.

Charles Manson was a homegrown American monster. What that monster did and how he did it is the subject of what follows.

# Chapter One

# Manson's Early Life

*"A baby is born into this world in a state of fear."*

—Charles Manson

Manson's mother, Kathleen Maddox, was just 15 years old when she became pregnant to a 23-year old petty criminal named Colonel Scott. Scott was not in the military (Colonel was his given name), but he liked to pretend that he was. Kathleen likely met Scott at one of the roadhouse clubs she frequented on the Ohio border.

When Scott disappeared, Kathleen was left in an undesirable situation. Kathleen's mother was a strict Christian, a follower of the Church of Nazarene, who insisted Kathleen raise her child within the church. Kathleen rebelled and decided to find another man to marry instead. The man whom Kathleen would marry at age 15, around halfway through her pregnancy, was 25-year-old William Manson.

From the moment of Charles Manson's birth on November 12, 1934, in Cincinnati, Ohio, he was marked as an outcast. At first, Manson was listed as "no name" but later William Manson was added to the baby's birth certificate, and he was subsequently given the name Charles. Following Charles' birth, Kathleen returned to her old ways, making money by running scams on men she met in bars. In 1937, William filed for divorce from Kathleen, stating "gross neglect of duties." Kathleen was unable or unwilling to care for two-year-old Manson. In a story Manson told later, Kathleen once tried to trade the infant to a waitress in exchange for a pitcher of beer.

In 1939, police arrested Kathleen for the robbery of a man named Frank Martin. She was sentenced to five years in jail, and Manson went to live with his highly religious aunt and uncle in West Virginia, who found him to be a badly behaved child and a compulsive liar. When Kathleen was granted parole three years later, she reclaimed her now eight-year-old son and went to work in a grocery store to support him.

Kathleen remarried in 1943 to a man named Lewis, who she had met at Alcoholics Anonymous. Lewis had no patience with Manson whose bad behavior had escalated into petty criminality, and in 1947, Lewis convinced Kathleen to send Manson to a minimum-security reform school in Indiana. Manson ran away from school after less than a year and went on a crime spree, breaking into a number of stores. When caught, authorities sent Manson to a different reform school, but he did the same thing, this time stealing a car he used to drive to Illinois where he got hold of a gun and committed armed robberies.

Now authorities sent Manson to Indiana Boys School, a strict facility where the young inmates were routinely beaten and forced to perform farm labor. It is here that Manson said older boys sexually abused him and that the abuse was encouraged by one of the staff members. The boys raped Manson so frequently he disassociated from the abuse and later described rape as "no big deal." Manson was small in stature, and the only way he could defend himself was with what he described as the "insane game," where he would flail his body wildly as though possessed and screech in such a way that his rapists would be frightened off.

In January 1952, just a month before he was eligible for parole, school wardens caught 17-year-old Manson raping another boy at knifepoint, and he lost his right to parole. Authorities transferred Manson to the Federal Reformatory in Petersburg, Virginia then to the maximum-security reformatory at Chillicothe, Ohio. Dedicating the next few years of his sentence to self-improvement, Manson was released on good behavior in mid-1954. Life came full circle for Manson when he returned to live under the watchful eye of his aunt and uncle in West Virginia, just as he had when he was two years old and his mother was in jail.

Manson started attending Nazarene church services with his family. The church's teachings, such as that women are inferior to men and that the path to salvation lies in renouncing material possessions, struck a chord with Manson, even though he continued his criminal ways and quickly developed a reputation as the bad boy in town.

In January 1955, Manson married a local woman named Rosalie Jean Willis. At the time, Rosalie falsely believed that she was pregnant, but within a few months of her wedding, she really was. The newlyweds decided to relocate to California, where Manson's mother was now living. They made the journey in a stolen car, and a few months after the Mansons started their new life in California, police arrested Manson for driving another stolen vehicle. Rosalie gave birth to Charles Manson, Jr. in March 1956, and in April his father was incarcerated at Terminal Island, San Pedro.

Though Rosalie visited Manson in prison during the first year of his sentence, her visits soon stopped. Manson felt betrayed when he learned that Rosalie had found another man to father their child, and when she served him with divorce papers in March 1957, he tried to escape from prison. Perhaps this abrupt severing of ties between Manson and his wife fueled his growing hatred of women. Newly single and with a lot of time to kill, Manson dedicated himself to studying the criminal world and began drawing together the sources that would form the basis of his cult.

# Chapter Two

# Becoming Charles Manson

*"The mind is endless. You put me in a dark solitary cell, and to you that's the end, to me it's the beginning, it's the universe in there, there's a world in there, and I'm free."*

—Charles Manson

While incarcerated at Terminal Island, Manson befriended the resident pimps. From these prostitution professionals, Manson learned how to select women to pimp out and how to control them. Manson was particularly interested in the pimps' insistence that women who had lived through traumatic experiences made the best prostitutes, and that with just a tiny bit of encouragement and care Manson could convince these women to do his bidding. Separating the women from any friends and family who might try to remove them from their situation was also key, the pimps said, and it was necessary to beat the women and take their possessions so that they became entirely dependent.

Manson's prison education didn't just come from pimps. While at Terminal Island, he underwent aptitude tests and while he had a slightly higher than average IQ, he was almost illiterate. Prison educators thought that Manson might benefit from a four-week course influenced by Dale Carnegie's famous book, *How to Win Friends and Influence People.*

The Carnegie Method distills all human endeavors down to two motivating factors: sexual desire and the desire for greatness. This method became like a religion to Manson. Never before had any worldview resonated so deeply with Manson, who himself desired pure admiration from those around him, particularly women. These two distinct but connected sources—the pimps of Terminal Island and Dale Carnegie—provided Manson with clear instructions on how to use sex as a tool and how to exert control over women.

With a plan emerging in his mind, Manson transformed himself into a model prisoner, and in 1958 he was released from prison seven months early. Although Manson was still on parole, he immediately set himself up as a pimp and was soon arrested for cheque fraud. He had already managed to manipulate one of the prostitutes working for him, 16-year-old Candy Stevens, into unquestioning loyalty, and she testified at his trial that she was pregnant and that they were going to be married, a testimony that bought Manson a ten-year suspended sentence. The couple were indeed married, but Manson's freedom didn't last long.

In June 1961, authorities revoked Manson's parole when police arrested him for trafficking prostitutes over state borders. Manson was driving Candy and another woman from California to New Mexico in violation of the Mann Act. He was then ordered to serve out his ten-year sentence at McNeil Federal Prison in Washington State.

Now 26, Manson had spent the majority of his life from the age of 12 onwards in the prison system. He felt more and more like an outcast in the free world. Unable to meet the demands of so-called normal society, Manson felt at home in prison amongst what he came to think of as his own people—the criminal underclass of the world.

Manson had played guitar for years, and he spent time jamming with other musicians on his ward, developing the musical skills he would come to believe guaranteed him ultimate stardom. His unrealistic dream to become bigger than the Beatles, who were at that time at the height of their American invasion, was fueled by a fellow inmate, Phil Kauffman. Kauffman had some vague experience in the L.A. music scene and promised Manson that he would get him a session with a producer at the music division of Universal Studios. This casual invitation warped in Manson's mind and he became convinced that there was a man in L.A. who was going to make him a superstar.

While serving time at McNeil Prison, Manson also became embroiled with a quasi-religious group that had a major influence on his later role as a cult leader—Scientologists. Again, prison authorities encouraged Manson's education. As with Dale Carnegie, the pimps, the Nazarene Church, and pop music, Manson took what he wanted from the information offered and used it to form a doctrine of his own. Manson's main takeaway from Scientology was the belief that we are all immortal beings trapped in human bodies on this planet we call earth. Life on earth is just a sliver of our potential experience and so to die is simply to move on. Manson would later use this skewed Scientology-based moral perspective as justification to convince his followers to kill.

In March 1967, Manson became eligible for release and, tellingly, tried to reject attempts to set him free. Manson didn't know how to survive in the real world and had settled into a kind of contentment in prison. Despite the fact that Manson was completely institutionalized, he was released on March 21, 1967, a free man with absolutely no idea of where to go or what to do.

Manson ended up in Berkeley, spending his days wandering the campus of UC Berkeley and his nights sleeping rough. The world had changed dramatically during the time Manson had been in jail. The sexual revolution was well underway, and politicized rebellion had become a central part of youth culture, particularly on university campuses. Young people from all over the state flooded into the Bay area looking for free love and a place where they could live as they chose, away from the restrictive, straight drudgery of their parents' generation.

It was easy for men to exploit the attempts of the young women to explore love and sexuality outside of marriage while embracing the drug culture of the time. Women looking for relationships, or sex, that didn't lead directly to their domestic servitude were easy prey for men whose intentions were not always as pure. Manson saw opportunity in these young runaways.

But another social movement, the civil rights movement, alarmed Manson. Used to the highly segregated world of prison culture, Manson saw the civil rights movement as a direct threat to what he saw as legitimate white supremacy. The Black Panthers frightened Manson, and he came to believe that a civil race war was on the horizon.

# Chapter Three

# Starting the Manson Family

*"I don't wanna take my time going to work, I got a motorcycle and a sleeping bag and ten or fifteen girls. What the hell I wanna go off and go to work for? Work for what?"*

—Charles Manson

Manson was not accustomed to living on the streets and was in need of a warm bed. At the UC Berkeley library, Manson met Mary Brunner, a library assistant who up to that point was living an ordinary life. Manson moved into Mary's apartment and spent his time taking day trips out to the Haight-Ashbury neighborhood of San Francisco.

LSD was legal at the time and many young women in San Francisco, who had escaped the rigid gender roles of the life they had left, embraced the drug culture. But for many, the promised utopia of the Bay was simply a more insular version of the subjugation they had left behind. Men used and abused women freely, and unplanned pregnancies and venereal disease reached epidemic levels. Drug dealers were also able to take advantage of young women who were far from home and starving and disillusioned with the scene.

Manson's arrival in the Haight directly coincided with the Summer of Love; the streets were alive with impressionable young people, looking for someone to give them answers. Manson developed a strategy for attracting an audience by sitting alone in a park somewhere and playing his guitar and singing. Once he had a few interested women sitting around him, he'd launch into his guru act, proselytizing that the answer these women were looking for lay within him. Manson promised to lead these women to true enlightenment but told them that was only possible if they renounced their possessions and their individuality and submitted entirely to his will.

Next Manson took his guru act to Venice Beach where he met his first true follower (not counting Mary Brunner who was still supporting Manson financially). Eighteen-year-old Lynette Fromme, who would become known as "Squeaky," was charmed by Manson, who told her he was known as "The Gardener" for his work taking care of flower children. Lynette returned to Berkeley with Manson, and with Mary the new threesome moved into an apartment in San Francisco.

There Manson was able to convince an old acquaintance to give him a piano, which he traded in for a Volkswagen minibus. Now able to take his guru act on the road, Manson attracted the attention of another woman, Patricia Krenwinkel, on Manhattan Beach in 1967. Krenwinkel later said that Manson was the first person who had ever told her she was beautiful and that she had sex with him on the first night they met. Thoroughly transfixed by Manson and desperate to become one of his girls, Krenwinkel left her job, car, apartment, and last paycheck behind and returned with the budding family to

San Francisco. Krenwinkel gave Manson her father's credit card and the foursome survived for a while by stealing and writing bad checks.

Susan "Sadie" Atkins was the next woman to join the Manson Family. Atkins was an ex-convict who was supporting herself by topless dancing. Manson was drawn to Atkins when he learned that she had danced in a cabaret led by the self-styled leader of the Satanic Church, Anton LaVey. Atkins was a heavy drug-user when she met Manson and was easily convinced to join his family and to set about recruiting more members, preferably male. Atkins was able to lure Bruce Davis to join the family in the fall of 1967, the first male member and a man who was later described as Manson's right-hand man.

Davis met the family when they were in Oregon. Manson had traded his minibus for a full-size yellow school bus and had taken his family on a tour of the American West; he had decided the family should move to Los Angeles. The Haight had become too dangerous, Manson said, life would be better for the family in L.A. What he didn't tell his family was that the real reason he wanted to move to Los Angeles was to pursue his dreams of stardom. Charles Manson was looking for a record deal.

# Chapter Four

# Seeking Fame in Los Angeles

*"If I had a desire, it would be to be free from desire."*

—Charles Manson

Los Angeles had long been a place of pilgrimage for people with dreams of stardom, but in the 1960s the city was also a hotbed of social unrest. The civil rights movement's first major rebellion took place in L.A. with the Watts Riot, instigated by police brutality against a black man. The city's young generation of actors and rock musicians were politically vocal, and youth culture as a whole was pushing back against a post-war America where the white middle classes were growing richer by the day while minorities were being pushed to the fringes of society.

Manson had no desire at all to level the social playing field or improve race relations, but he did convince his followers that the best way to spread his message to the world would be with a record deal. In 1967, Manson was 34 years old and essentially unemployable due to his criminal record. Manson believed that his talent was enough to transform his life and that fame and fortune were his for the taking.

Incredibly, Manson did have an audition with a producer in the music division of Universal Studios named Gary Stromberg. Manson's friend from jail, Phil Kauffman, had contacted Stromberg, and he agreed to give Manson some studio time to record a demo. Arriving at the studio barefoot and with his four obedient girls by his side, Manson impressed Stromberg, but once he got in front of the microphone, he deflated. Manson had no idea how to behave in a recording studio and was unable to produce anything that showed Stromberg he had any talent.

At the end of the painful three-hour session, Stromberg sent Manson away telling him to continue to work on his music and that he'd perhaps invite him back to try again sometime. Manson misinterpreted this brush-off and believed he had another shot at stardom; he just had to practice. Stromberg was guilty of leading Manson on; at the time, Universal was flirting with the idea of making a film about the second coming of Christ, set amongst modern-day L.A. counter-culture, and Stromberg treated the Manson Family as research.

But Stromberg soon tired of Manson, and it became clear that there would be no record deal with Universal. Manson kept up his act, telling his family that Stromberg didn't get his message and didn't deserve his talent. The family moved on to Topanga Canyon and settled in a wreck of a house called the Spiral Staircase, famous for being a community center of sorts for the area's spiritual gurus and minor cults. The Spiral Staircase was a hangout for L.A.'s rich and famous icons of counter-culture. Jim Morrison, members of the Mamas and the Papas, and Jay Sebring were all said to get high at the Spiral Staircase, and Manson was drawn by the place's starry reputation.

However, the Manson Family stayed at Spiral Staircase for just two months. Manson didn't like the other gurus who represented competition for his girls' affection and pulled away from the satanic and sex fetish elements of what went on at Spiral Staircase. Manson piled his family back into the school bus and, with the Beatles' *Magical Mystery Tour* as their soundtrack, drove them through the Mojave Desert.

In the winter of 1967, Manson attracted a new follower. Fourteen-year-old Diane Lake had grown up on a commune called Hog Farm and had her parents' permission when she joined the Manson Family. Diane was Manson's favorite for the first year she was with him, and while he continued to have sex with all of his girls, he chose Diane most often. It's unclear how long Manson had been physically abusing Mary, the mother of his child and ostensibly the very first Manson girl, but once Diane was on the scene it seems Manson took out his frustration on Mary more often. Mary could often be seen sporting a black eye, and it was Manson's brutalizing of Mary that left the other girls afraid of his temper.

All of the girls were forced to scavenge for food to survive. Manson had watched the young runaways of the Haight survive on what society threw away. These "Diggers" as they called themselves were always female and were forced to not only scavenge for food in dumpsters but also to prepare and serve the food to the men. Manson's followers often resorted to having sex with supermarket and restaurant workers in exchange for food for the family.

The whole family also began having group sex around this time. Manson would give his family large doses of LSD then preach to them for hours. Sometimes he would play his guitar, encouraging the family to sing along to his songs, and often these sessions would end with Manson orchestrating an orgy. Manson would be in complete control of these group sessions, even talking each member through what he wanted them to do and to whom.

The Manson Family numbered around two dozen at this time. It seems there was no shortage of young men and women arriving in Topanga Canyon desperate to join the community. New male recruits were immediately welcomed, but Manson forced female recruits to endure an initiation process. During the initiation—or interrogation—he would take the aspiring Manson girl into a room alone and stay with her for days, breaking down her emotional and physical barriers by forcing her to confront painful memories and continually have sex with him.

It was around this time that Deirdre Shaw was welcomed into the family. Deirdre was not forced to go through Manson's abusive initiation process for the simple reason that she had money. Deirdre was the daughter of an actress, Angela Lansbury, and let the Manson Family use her mother's credit card. Once

Lansbury canceled the credit card, Manson also canceled Deirdre's invitations to hang out with the Manson Family.

A second famous person became involved with the Manson Family around the spring of 1968. Two of the Manson girls, Patricia and Ella Jo, were hitch-hiking on the Pacific Coast Highway when Beach Boy Dennis Wilson picked them up and invited them to his house. The girls complied, and after spending an afternoon with Dennis, they returned to Manson and told him about their famous new friend. Over subsequent days, Manson managed to worm his way into Dennis' life, taking advantage of his extreme generosity to move his family into Dennis' house. Manson also hoped that Dennis would be able to help him boost his music career, a dream Manson had never let go.

But any opportunities Dennis threw Manson's way, he squandered. It became clear to anyone with musical training that Manson could only play a few chords on his guitar and none of his songs were good enough to record. After a few months, Dennis was desperate to part ways with Manson and even moved out of his own home, leaving his landlord to deal with evicting the Manson Family.

# Chapter Five

# Spahn Ranch and Helter Skelter

*"When I get to the bottom I go back to the top of the slide
Where I stop and I turn and I go for a ride
Till I get to the bottom and I see you again."*

—The Beatles, "Helter Skelter"

In the late summer of 1968, the Manson Family moved to Spahn Ranch, a dilapidated Western movie set in Chatsworth at the base of the Santa Susana Mountains. Spahn Ranch had been a working movie set since the silent film era, but in recent years the ranch had fallen into disrepair. The ranch's 80-year-old owner, George Spahn, survived by hiring out horses to tourists looking for a taste of the old Wild West.

Over the next year, the now three-dozen strong family camped out among the caves and rotten wooden shacks of Spahn Ranch. Spahn was an invalid and nearly blind, and the family was able to squat on his land without him even realizing for some time. Eventually, one of the Manson girls asked if the family could stay on Spahn's land for free if they agreed to do some maintenance. The owner agreed and told his ranch hands, Shorty Shea and Juan Flynn, to direct the motley crew to complete long-outstanding tasks around the ranch. One of the girls, Lynette Fromme, was assigned to Spahn's home as a housekeeper and caregiver.

The ranch still operated as a movie set from time to time, attracting producers of low-budget western movies and TV shows to shoot outdoor scenes there. Whenever a production crew arrived, the Manson family girls would flirt with the team and beg for food. Shea and Flynn quickly realized that Manson was manipulating Spahn to his own ends and that he was trying to convince him to leave the ranch to the family in his will. Shea, in particular, made it his mission to get rid of the Manson Family and tried to convince Spahn to sell the ranch.

At Spahn Ranch, Manson's orchestrated acid-fueled sermon and orgies, which increased in frequency and intensity. The family listened to Manson's philosophical ramblings for hours, even as they became more anti-Semitic, racist, and violent than ever before. In late 1968, Manson seized upon a new text for his prophecies: a musical training manual designed to help him create an army out of his cult—the Beatles' 1968 album known as "the White Album."

Manson said that the Beatles had channeled his own teachings and used them to create the White Album, which he saw as a vehicle for sharing those teachings with the world. Whether Manson truly believed this fanciful idea is difficult to discern, but his starving, acid-frazzled followers believed it wholeheartedly. According to Manson, the White Album expressed the Beatles' need for a spiritual savior and contained coded messages explicitly directed at him. Manson was, he believed, the savior the Beatles were looking for. Manson also used the coincidence of the Beatle's song "Sexy Sadie," his nickname for follower Susan Atkins, to prove his point and focused on the lyrics of "Piggies," a song about class struggle, assuring his followers that they were the piggies the Beatles were writing about.

To the family, Manson's explanation of the White Album made his other, even more fantastical predictions about the future seem legitimate. Of course Manson didn't get his own recording contract; he was spreading his message through the Beatles instead. Manson also used other popular music of the day to convince the family that they had now entered the most crucial stage of their journey. These were the days of Helter Skelter.

According to Manson, America was on the brink of an apocalyptic race war. In the summer of 1969, Manson said, the black population of America was going to unite and rise up in arms against the white population. The Beatles' song "Helter Skelter" was named after a rollercoaster in England, yet Manson assured his followers that it was, in fact, named after the coming race war. Once the race war began, Manson said, he and his followers would retire to the desert. There, in Death Valley, the family would find an underground city where they could escape the war and wait for the Beatles to join them.

Manson taught his followers that although the black population would easily overpower the white population in war, once the planet belonged to them, they wouldn't know how to sustain it. At this point, the Manson Family could emerge from their underground kingdom, enslave the black population, and become the rulers of the world. Of course, re-populating the earth after Helter Skelter would be of paramount importance, and Manson taught the women in his family that his complete control over who they had sex with and when was all part of this master plan.

It's impossible to tell if Manson truly believed in what he was teaching, but his family did. Preparations for war began on New Year's Eve, 1969. Manson put his followers through a vigorous regime of what he referred to as "desert survival." Followers were deprived of food and water and given knives and guns, which they needed to learn how to use. Sometime soon, Manson said, a group of black men was going to start Helter Skelter by invading the house of some rich Hollywood family and killing everyone inside, writing messages on the walls in blood. This would be the family's sign, Manson said, to escape to their underground city in the desert.

Before the family could escape the war, Manson said, he had to release a record in response to the Beatles' White Album, telling the pop stars how to find them. To do that, Manson had to enlist the support of Terry Melcher, a prominent Hollywood record executive and the son of Doris Day. At that time, Melcher was in a relationship with Candice Bergen, an actress who lived with Melcher at the now notorious address of 10050 Cielo Drive.

Bergen and Melcher lived a lavish lifestyle as Hollywood royalty but liked to slum it from time to time with the local hippies. During a visit to the Manson Family at Spahn Ranch, Melcher took a liking to the 17-year-old Ruth Ann Moorehouse. Impressed by Manson's intensity and the respect given to him by his harem of young girls, Melcher began spending more and more time at Spahn Ranch. Movie producer Greg Jacobson was vaguely considering filming a documentary about Manson, and he and Melcher thought they could make money out of Manson's extreme counter-cultural scene.

Melcher did, however, draw the line at inviting Manson or any members of his family to his home at Cielo Drive, and it soon became clear to Manson that no record contract would be forthcoming from his company. And as Melcher's personal life fell apart, he withdrew completely from the social scene and moved out of his house at Cielo Drive.

In March 1969, Melcher agreed to visit Spahn Ranch one last time to decide whether Manson had what it takes to be a rock star. This was a huge mistake. Manson and the family spent weeks preparing for this important meeting, but when the time came, Melcher didn't show. Manson was livid and vowed to hunt Melcher down and punish him for his slight.

# Chapter Six

# The First Murder

*"Believe me, if I started murdering people, there'd be none of you left."*

—Charles Manson

Manson turned up at 10050 Cielo Drive on March 23, 1969, intent on confronting Terry Melcher. Manson didn't know that Melcher had moved to Malibu and that the house was now being rented to Roman Polanski and his wife, Sharon Tate. The owner of the property, who was living in the guest house at the time, told Manson that Melcher had left and forced Manson to leave the property. Before he left, Manson looked up to the balcony of the house and saw Sharon Tate standing there. Manson stared at Sharon, and she stared right back.

In May 1969, Melcher agreed to visit Spahn Ranch again, and this time he showed up. Melcher listened to Manson's music and promised him a recording session with a friend who owned a mobile recording studio in a van. Melcher returned in June with the recording van, but the entire day was a disaster, and Melcher declined to support Manson any further.

Now Manson was angrier than ever and pushed the Manson Family into another turning point; what began as training exercises for a race war that most of the family treated as light-hearted games evolved into serious crimes. The family had been going on so-called creepy crawls for some months already; night-time excursions where family members crawled into homes belonging to the rich and famous just to rearrange the furniture and laugh at the chaos their trick caused the next morning. Now these creepy crawls became thefts, with credit cards being the preferred loot.

Around this time, Bobby Beausoleil began spending time with the Manson Family. Beausoleil had acted in Kenneth Anger's film *Lucifer Rising* and joined several rock bands in recent years. When Beausoleil met Manson, he was staying with Gary Hinman, a music teacher who lived in Topanga Canyon and allowed various hippies and social outcasts to crash at his home. Manson saw an opportunity in Beausoleil and encouraged him to spend time at Spahn Ranch. Beausoleil was good-looking and charismatic and could attract pretty girls to join the Manson Family even if he himself was too self-assured to submit to Manson's will.

Beausoleil dutifully brought his numerous girlfriends to the ranch, and girls like Gypsy and Leslie Van Houten joined the family full-time. Beausoleil also brought Gary Hinman to Manson's attention. Hinman was a Buddhist and would not join Manson's Family but was generous with his possessions, cars, and drugs.

By the summer of 1969, Manson was so desperate to get some cash together to kick-start Helter Skelter and his family's escape to the desert that he decided to start a drug-dealing operation. Manson's follower and right-hand man Charles "Tex" Watson set up a bad deal, promising $2,500 worth of weed to a dealer known as Lotsa Poppa in exchange for the cash. He took the cash but had no weed. Poppa threatened the Manson Family, saying that he was a member of the Black Panthers, and if his money were not returned, he and his fellow Panthers would come to Spahn Ranch and kill everyone there. In retaliation, Manson drove to Poppa's home and shot him in the chest. He survived but never reported the assault to police.

When Manson relayed what he had done to his family, the atmosphere at Spahn Ranch became desperate. Now it wasn't just Manson's failure to get a record deal and the crushing poverty at Spahn Ranch that was making life unbearable; there was also the threat of annihilation by Black Panthers to contend with. At the same time, Beausoleil got into trouble with a biker gang who hung out at Spahn Ranch. Beausoleil had sold mescaline manufactured by Gary Hinman to the bikers, who reported that the drugs were actually poison. They wanted their money back.

Manson convinced Beausoleil to confront Hinman and demand from him not only the drug money but anything else of value he possessed. Beausoleil drove with Bruce Davis, Susan Atkins, and Mary Brunner to Hinman's house on July 25, 1969. At the house, Beausoleil pulled a gun on Hinman when he refused to give back the money. There was nothing wrong with the mescaline, Hinman said. Susan kept the gun on Hinman while

Beausoleil searched the house, but Hinman managed to overpower her, causing Beausoleil to beat him.

Eventually, Davis drove back to Spahn Ranch to pick up Manson, who wanted to take part in what was to follow. Manson brought a sword and used it to slash Hinman's face and cut off part of his ear. After Manson left, Beausoleil continued to beat Hinman over the course of the night and into the next day, with Susan and Mary still present. Hinman maintained that he had no money and threatened to call the police as soon as they left.

Beausoleil called Manson to tell him about Hinman's threat, and Manson ordered him to kill Hinman, making the murder look as though the Black Panthers did it in retaliation for the shooting of Lotsa Poppa. Beausoleil stabbed Hinman to death and used his blood to write the phrase "political piggy" on the wall. Beausoleil, Susan, and Mary tried to remove their fingerprints from Hinman's home before they drove away in his cars. It took two weeks before anyone found Hinman's body.

Beausoleil tried to distance himself from the Manson Family after he murdered Gary Hinman and drove to San Francisco, leaving his pregnant girlfriend, Kitty, behind. Beausoleil drove in one of the cars he had stolen from Hinman, the very car in which he had stashed the bloody knife. When the car broke down, police were called to the scene. They examined the car, quickly finding the knife. Police arrested Beausoleil and matched his fingerprints to those found at Hinman's home. Beausoleil was booked for homicide, and on April 18, 1970, 22-year-old Beausoleil was found guilty of first-degree murder and sentenced to death. When the California Supreme Court ruled the death penalty unconstitutional in 1972, authorities commuted Beausoleil's sentence to life in prison.

# Chapter Seven

# 10050 Cielo Drive

*"Woman, I have no mercy for you."*

—Susan "Sadie" Atkins

Manson trusted no one, including Bobby Beausoleil, and decided the only way he could move ahead with Helter Skelter was to break him out of jail. But when news reached Manson that two more of his followers, Mary Brunner and Sandra Good, had been arrested for using a stolen credit card, he lost it. The family couldn't afford the bail, and these recent arrests served only to convince Manson further that straight society was out to destroy everything he had created. Someone was going to have to pay.

In the foothills and valleys of Los Angeles, August 1969 was a painfully hot month. With the mercury reaching over 100 degrees Fahrenheit, the Manson Family suffered out at Spahn Ranch. On the opposite end of the social spectrum, actress Sharon Tate was suffering too. Whiling away the days in her mansion at 10050 Cielo Drive, Sharon was almost nine months pregnant and without her husband, Roman Polanski who was shooting a movie in London.

Sharon did have house guests to keep her company, though. Abigail Folger, the heiress to the Folger Coffee Company and her boyfriend, Wojciech Frykowski, were also living at Cielo Drive. On the evening of August 8, 1969, Sharon made phone calls to her sister and her friend to cancel plans she had made, saying that she was tired and would spend the night in with another friend, Jay Sebring. The foursome, Sharon, Jay, Abigail, and Wojciech, ate at a local Mexican restaurant before returning to Sharon's home at Cielo Drive.

At 11.30 pm, Manson took his trusted follower Tex Watson to one side and explained to him what he had to do. For the good of the family, Manson said, Tex had to lead the others to Cielo Drive to "totally destroy everyone in that house" and steal whatever they could. It's unclear whether Manson even knew who was now living in that particular house, but he must have known they were rich and that they would serve as an example to the rest of the world that no one was safe.

Manson rounded up Susan Atkins, Patricia Krenwinkel, and new follower Linda Kasabian. Dressed in black, the girls grabbed their knives and jumped into the car with Tex. Manson rested at Spahn Ranch, waiting for news from 10050 Cielo Drive.

When the group arrived at the house, Tex climbed a telephone pole and snipped the wire. It was only now that the group had arrived that Tex told the girls exactly what they were there to do. If the girls were shocked, they didn't show it, and they dutifully followed Tex's lead in what came next.

Steve Parent, an 18-year-old friend of the caretaker at Cielo Drive, was the first to be murdered. Parent was leaving the property in his car, having just visited his friend, when Tex shot him four times. Tex then entered the house through an open window and told the girls to follow him inside. New follower Kasabian was terrified and unable to help, so Tex told her to go back to the car and keep watch.

In the sitting room of the house, Tex woke Wojciech who had fallen asleep on the couch, and Susan ventured upstairs where she found Abigail reading in bed. Abigail saw Susan but wasn't alarmed at first. It wasn't unusual for strangers to be in the house. But when Susan brandished a large knife and told Abigail, Sharon, and Jay to go with her downstairs, the group were terrified.

Tex tied a rope around Wojciech's throat, threw it over a beam in the house, and tied it around Sharon's throat. Tex demanded money and grew furious when no one produced any, then he shot Jay in the stomach. As Sharon and Abigail screamed in terror, Tex stabbed Jay, over and over again. Realizing that no one was going to escape alive if he didn't do something, Wojciech tried to break free, causing Susan to attack him with a knife. Wojciech was able to overpower Susan, so Tex shot him twice then battered him with the handle of his gun. Incredibly, Wojciech still managed to escape the house, but Tex caught up with him on the lawn and ended his life with a knife.

Abigail also broke free of Patricia, but she caught her and stabbed her repeatedly. Tex finally ended Abigail's life with his knife. Sharon was the only person still alive in the house; she pleaded for her life and the life of her unborn child. As Sharon begged, Susan Atkin's began stabbing her, being sure to stab her directly through her pregnant stomach. Later, Susan said she "got sick of listening to her so I stabbed her and then I just stabbed her and she fell and I stabbed her again, just kept stabbing and stabbing."

The group almost left without writing the bloody graffiti Manson had explicitly told them to leave behind. Susan went back into the house and used a towel to write "PIG" on the front door of 10500 Cielo Drive in the victims' blood.

The group returned to Spahn Ranch where Manson was upset to see them return so soon and with so little money. Manson drove back to Cielo Drive to "see what my children had done." Manson tampered with the crime scene, moving objects around and leaving objects behind in the hope that his random clues would baffle police but, like Tex, he didn't take anything of real value.

It was Sharon Tate's maid, Winifred Chapman, arriving to work at 8 am on August 9, who found the bodies and alerted the police. Police booked the house's 19-year-old caretaker, William Garretson, immediately. No one believed that Garretson could have been in the guesthouse the entire time and not have heard anything. Garretson was booked on five counts of murder and taken to the police station. This was a disaster for Manson. No one had put together the pieces that Manson thought he had clearly laid, linking this murder with that of Gary Hinman and to the Black Panthers.

The whole thing had been a failure, Manson said. The group was going to have to out a second night and do it all over again.

# Chapter Eight

# Rosemary and Leno LaBianca

*"Charlie was always preaching love. Charlie had no idea what love was. Charlie was so far from love it wasn't even funny. Death is Charlie's trip. It really is."*

—Paul Watkins

Rosemary and Leno LaBianca were a middle-aged, married couple who lived at 3301 Waverly Drive in the Los Feliz area of L.A. Leno worked as a supermarket executive, and when members of the Manson Family pulled up outside their home on the evening of August 10, 1969, he and his wife were getting ready to go to bed.

Manson had not been physically present for the murders at Cielo Drive, although he did go to the house before the police found the crime scene to set-dress it. This time, he was a part of the group who turned up at 3301 Waverly Drive. Manson and Tex entered the house first through an unlocked back door. They found Leno, like Wojciech in the Tate house the night before, asleep on the couch. Manson told Tex to bring Rosemary from the bedroom and to cover the couple's heads with pillowcases and to bind them in place, which he did.

Manson robbed the LaBiancas first, taking Rosemary's purse from her. Next, he collected Patricia Krenwinkel and Leslie Van Houten from the car and brought them into the house, giving Tex the horrifying instruction to "make sure everybody does something." Then Manson got back in the car and drove away from the LaBianca home with Linda Kasabian, Susan Atkins, and Clem Grogan inside.

Inside the house, Tex Watson killed Leno LaBianca by stabbing him in the throat multiple times with a bayonet. He then used his bayonet on Rosemary who was trying to fight off Patricia and Lesley. Patricia stabbed Rosemary again when Tex, heeding Manson's instruction that everyone should take part in the murders, told Leslie to take over. Leslie stabbed Rosemary LaBianca 16 times. Tex carved the word "WAR" into Leno's stomach before all three murderers wrote the words "Rise," "Death to pigs," and "Healter Skelter (sic)" on the walls in blood. As a parting gesture, Patricia stabbed Leno's corpse with a carving fork, which she left jutting out of his stomach alongside the steak knife she left in his neck.

While all of this had been going on, Manson was driving the other family members around Los Angeles. Manson bought them chocolate milkshakes with Rosemary LaBianca's money then had Linda ditch Rosemary's wallet in the hope that a black person would find it and incriminate themselves in the LaBianca murders.

But the killing still wasn't over. Manson pressed the others to find out if they knew anyone in the Venice Beach area they were driving through. Linda Kasabian admitted to knowing an actor who lived nearby. Manson handed Linda a knife and told her to knock on this actor's door and stab him. Manson also gave his gun to Clem, instructing him to shoot the actor if Linda was unable to stab him to death. Faced with the task of murdering an innocent man, Linda balked and told the others that she couldn't remember where the actor lived. Manson drove back to Spahn Ranch, and the rest of the gang hitchhiked back.

Meanwhile, police had realized that the man they had in custody for the murders at 10050 Cielo Drive, William Garretson, was not involved and moved on to a theory involving a drug deal gone wrong. The LAPD didn't initially think the murders at Cielo Drive and Waverly Street were connected. Manson praised his followers for their work but was dismayed that none of the news coverage even hinted that the killers were black. If things carried on as they were, there would be no race war and no escape to the desert.

# Chapter Nine

# Catching Charles Manson

*"I'm nobody. I'm a tramp, a bum, a hobo. I'm a boxcar and a jug of wine, and a straight razor if you get too close to me."*

—Charles Manson

For months after the Manson Family murders, no one had any idea that Charlie Manson and his followers were involved. The only member of the Manson Family who seemed in the least bit perturbed by the murders was Linda Kasabian, a relatively new member of the family who had stayed out in the car during the killings at 10050 Cielo Drive. Linda had fled Spahn Ranch a few days after the murders, leaving her baby daughter behind.

Los Angeles County police raided Spahn Ranch on Saturday, August 16, 1969, believing the ranch to be the headquarters of an auto theft ring. The police searched the ranch for hours and arrested everyone they found. The Manson Family spent just two nights in jail, thanks to an invalid warrant, and returned to Spahn Ranch to confront Shorty Shea, whom Manson believed had called the police. Police had confiscated the family's cars during the raid, and Social Services had taken all the children living on Spahn Ranch. Linda Kasabian appealed to Social Services to get her child back but told no one what she knew about the murders. Not yet.

On August 26, Shorty Shea got into a car, most likely with Manson, Bruce Davis, Tex Watson, and Clem Grogan, and was never seen alive again. When his remains were discovered some eight years later, the body showed signs of having been subjected to brutal torture and multiple stab wounds. Manson implicated himself in his disappearance by falsely telling the other ranch hands that Shea had gone to San Francisco. Manson was more concerned about his bad relations with a local biker gang and the war he erroneously believed he had started with the Black Panthers than the police. Yet he knew that if he wanted to keep his family under his spell, he had to isolate them further.

At the end of August 1969, the Manson Family finally started to put their plan to move into the desert into action. The family swapped Spahn Ranch for Barker Ranch and Myers Ranch located just south of the town of Ballarat in Death Valley. Here, Manson worked his followers to the bone, ordering them to build hidden bunkers and dig holes to hide supplies. Each night, Manson continued to dose his followers with acid and deliver lengthy sermons about the coming apocalypse.

Manson admitted to murder during these sermons, adding threats to any followers who might be considering defecting. Susan Atkins also boasted about her involvement in the murders. This scared younger and newer followers who wanted to leave the Manson Family behind but were trapped by the desert that surrounded them. Out in the desert, the Manson Family also started to run out of the two of the things they desperately needed to survive: food and acid.

Life in the Manson Family became harsh and frightening. Two girls were so desperate to escape that they walked for 16 hours across the desert before they were able to hitch a ride into Los Angeles. Manson warned the family that he would hunt deserters down and kill them, and one of the girls who had escaped disappeared soon after. An unidentified corpse that matched her description turned up in a river near Mulholland Drive in November 1969, stabbed 157 times.

The next deserter was Tex Watson, Manson's right-hand man. Tex had had enough of working in the desert and searching for a mythical hole that would lead the family to the underground city awaiting them. He didn't want to take orders from Manson anymore and escaped in his car to Los Angeles where he took a flight back home to Texas. Eventually, Tex would attempt to return to the family, but by that time, they would have left Barker Ranch behind.

Stephanie Schram and Kitty Lusinger, who was pregnant with Bobby Beausoleil's child, were also more than ready to leave and fled Barker Ranch in October 1969. The next morning, while the pair was still lost in the desert, police raided Barker Ranch. Death Valley park rangers had run the license plates on a few of the Manson Family's vehicles and realized they were stolen. Police arrested 11 followers on charges of auto theft and arson. As police drove away from the ranch, they noticed two girls walking in the desert. Stephanie and Kitty told police that they were trying to escape the family and were afraid for their lives; they were taken into protective custody.

Manson was in Los Angeles during the first raid but was arrested when police returned a second time. Now, 27 family members were in custody, and it was only a matter of time before police put the pieces together. When police interviewed Susan Atkins about the murder of Gary Hinman, she bragged openly about her involvement but said that Manson was not involved. When Susan told her prison cellmates all about the family, Helter Skelter, and her involvement in the murders in 10050 Cielo Drive, she sealed her fate. Susan's cellmates were horrified and called police in Hollywood to tell them everything Susan had said.

On December 1, 1969, the LAPD broke the news to the world. A hippy clan, now known as the Manson Family, were the chief suspects in the murders at 10050 Cielo Drive and the LaBianca residence. A young district attorney, Vincent Bugliosi, announced that he would prosecute the case against Charles Manson, Susan Atkins, Lesley Van Houten, and Patricia Krenwinkel on multiple charges of murder.

Key witnesses in the trial were former Manson followers Mary Brunner, Linda Kasabian, and Susan Atkins. Prosecutors promised Susan immunity from the death penalty for her role in the murders if she would agree to testify against the others. She agreed, but her story changed multiple times, and in front of the grand jury, she minimized her involvement in the murders and said that Manson was not involved at all.

# Chapter Ten
# Life and Death Behind Bars

*"You know, a long time ago being crazy meant something. Nowadays everybody's crazy."*

—Charles Manson

Manson treated the Manson Family trials like his own reality TV show. At first, Manson wanted to represent himself, but the judge quickly realized that Manson was unfit for the task and only intent on making scenes. Manson fired the first litigator assigned to his case and hired acquaintance Ronald Hughes before settling on the esteemed defense attorney Irving Kanarek. Manson, Susan, Leslie, and Patricia all disrupted pre-trial court proceedings with planned protests. When Susan fired her attorney and refused to testify against Manson, the prosecution became desperate to cement its case and offered Linda Kasabian full immunity for her testimony.

Charles Manson's trial finally began on June 15, 1970. Jury selection alone took five weeks. On Manson's very first day in court, he appeared with an "X" carved into his forehead, still dripping with fresh blood. In a statement, Manson claimed to have x-ed himself from the world, and within a week, the three Manson women on trial had also inflicted the cuts on their foreheads, as had other Manson Family members camped on the street outside.

Attorneys interrogated Linda Kasabian on the witness stand for a total of 18 days. The three Manson women on trial wanted to take the stand, but their defense team would not allow it, knowing that the women sought only to absolve Manson. When Manson took the stand, it was to deliver a long monologue about his difficult life. This monologue ended with Manson blaming every American person, particularly President Nixon, for the murders while claiming he himself had no responsibility for them.

The jury in the Manson trials deliberated for ten days and came back with the verdict of guilty on all charges for all four defendants. On March 26, 1971, the four defendants were sentenced to death. Tex Watson's trial had not yet begun, but he too would be found guilty of multiple murder and sentenced to death. However, all of the Manson Family's sentences were commuted to life when the state of California abolished the death penalty in 1972.

Manson was admitted to state prison for the last time on April 22, 1971. Seven counts of first-degree murder—of Abigail Folger, Wojciech Frykowski, Steven Parent, Sharon Tate, Jay Sebring, and Leno and Rosemary LaBianca—became nine when Manson was found guilty of murdering Gary Hinman and Shorty Shea in 1972.

Manson was a problematic prisoner from the beginning. No warden wanted responsibility for the most notorious murderer of the era. In an attempt to protect himself from the prison population, a large portion of which would like to see him dead, Manson joined the Aryan Brotherhood and adapted the cross on his forehead into a swastika.

When Vincent Bugliosi published *Helter Skelter: The True Story of the Manson Murders* in 1974, the book became an instant best-seller and gave Manson a second flush of global fame. Manson remained in the headlines throughout the 1980s by giving a series of television interviews. One interview for *CBS News Nightwatch* that aired in 1986 won the Emmy Award for Best Interview.

Manson was moved from jail to jail throughout the 1970s and '80s, spending stretches of time in Protective Housing Units to keep him safe from other prisoners. But in September 1984, Manson was seriously injured when a fellow inmate poured paint thinner on him and set him on fire.

Manson came up for parole and was denied a total of 12 times. The last time Manson was denied parole was in April 2012 at which time he was 77 years old. Charles Manson died on November 19, 2017 from cardiac arrest resulting from respiratory failure due to colon cancer. Manson died ten years before his next parole hearing, which was scheduled for 2027, by which time he would have been 92 years old.

# Conclusion

Charles Manson had his first son with his wife, Rosalie Jean Willis, in 1956. Although Charles Manson, Jr. did everything he could to distance himself from his father, even changing his name to Jay White, the burden of having a killer for a dad was ultimately too much. Jay White took his life in 1993, dying of a self-inflicted gunshot wound to the head. Manson himself lived on for another 24 years.

The death and destruction caused by Manson and his followers transcended the moment in which it was committed. The trauma of the Manson Murders did not only affect the families of the victims (and perpetrators) but a whole generation, many of whom saw the murders as the dark end of the Swinging Sixties. After what happened at Cielo Drive, Hollywood, hippie culture, and America itself would never be the same again.

Fascination with the Manson Murders has endured over the last five decades. The extreme violence involved in the murders, the senselessness and lack of motive and the randomness with which the killers chose their victims all served to intensify public disgust and interest. Yet, the most disturbing thing about the Manson Family Murders is not the bizarre otherness of those who carried them out but their ordinariness.

Charles Manson was a run-of-the-mill cult leader who used old-fashioned misogyny and racism to indoctrinate his followers. Far from being a hippie himself, Manson posed as a spiritual father figure to lure flower children into his cult and kept them there by using classic abuse techniques of isolation, manipulation, punishment, and reward. A notorious celebrity, instantly recognizable by his wild eyes and the swastika carved into his forehead, Manson holds a place in the cultural consciousness as the leader of all the cult leaders. Yet there was nothing at all extraordinary about Charles Manson.

All Manson ever really wanted was to be famous. In this, at least, he was successful.

Made in United States
North Haven, CT
22 August 2023